# BATS

# WRINKLE-FACED BATS

## Pamela J. Gerholdt
### ABDO & Daughters

Published by Abdo & Daughters, 4940 Viking Drive, Suite 622, Edina, Minnesota 55435.

Library bound edition distributed by Rockbottom Books, Pentagon Tower, P.O. Box 36036, Minneapolis, Minnesota 55435.

Printed in the United States.

Cover Photo credit: Animals Animals
Interior Photo credits: Animals Animals, page 17
Dr. Don Wilson pages 11, 9, 21
Merlin D. Tuttle 19

Edited by Julie Berg

## Library of Congress Cataloging-in-Publication

Gerholdt, Pamela J.
    Wrinkle-faced bat / by Pamela J. Gerholdt.
      p. cm. — (Bats)
Includes bibliographical references (p. 24) and index.
ISBN 1-56239-504-1
1. Wrinkle-faced bat—Juvenile literature. [1. Wrlnkle-faced bat. 2. Bats.]
I. Title. II. Series: Gerholdt, Pamela J. Bats.
QL737.C57G47 1995
599.4—dc20
                                95-7350
                                  CIP
                                  AC

## About The Author

Pam Gerholdt has had a lifelong interest in animals.  She is a member of the Minnesota Herpetological Society and is active in conservation issues.  She lives in Webster, Minnesota with her husband, sons, and assorted other animals.

Revised Edition 2002

# Contents

# WRINKLE-FACED BATS

There are over 900 **species** of bats in the world. Wrinkle-faced bats are called "New World" leaf-nosed bats because they are found in Central and South America. They have medium brown, dark brown, or yellow brown fur on their backs and the back of their heads, and a white spot on each shoulder. Their faces have no fur. As the name suggests, wrinkle-faced bats have wrinkled faces.

All bats are **mammals**, like dogs, cats, horses, and humans. But bats do something no other mammal can do—they can fly!

*Wrinkle-faced bats have no fur on their faces.*

# WHERE THEY'RE FOUND

Bats live on all of the world's **continents** except Antarctica, the **polar regions**, and a few ocean islands. Wrinkle-faced bats live in much of Central America and South America.

CENTRAL
AMERICA

*Wrinkle-faced bats live in much of Central America and South America.*

SOUTH
AMERICA

DETAIL
AREA

# WHERE THEY LIVE

Wrinkle-faced bats live in moist and dry areas, in forests and open areas. They **roost** under the leaves of mango and rayo trees. They roost alone, or in two's and three's, with never more that 12 bats in one tree.

Bats roost by hanging upside down by their feet. It's easy for them because they have five toes with sharp, curved claws, and knees that point backwards!

*Many bats roost by hanging upside down. This is a roosting dog-faced bat.*

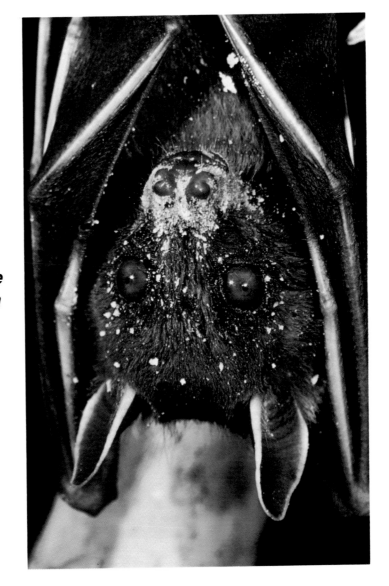

# SIZES

Most bats are 3 to 5 inches (7.5 to 12.5 cm) long and weigh 1 to 3.5 ounces (28 to 98 g). Wrinkle-faced bats only grow to just over 2.5 inches (6.5 cm) with a **wing span** of about 9 inches (22.5 cm). They weigh .5 to 1 ounce (14 to 28 g).

Some bats are even smaller, like the Kitti's hog-nosed bats. They only grow to 1 inch (2.5 cm) long—about the size of a large bumble bee. Although their bodies are small, their wing span is 6.5 inches (16.25 cm).

Flying foxes are much larger. They grow to over 16 inches (40 cm) long with a wing span over 5.5 feet (165 cm).

*Wrinkle-faced bats only grow to just over 2.5 inches (6.5 cm).*

# SHAPES

Bats come in many different shapes. Wrinkle-faced bats are among the strangest-looking bats. Their naked, short, wide faces are covered with extra skin that sticks out in wrinkled folds. When **roosting**, this bat covers its face with the chin fold that pulls up over the top of the bat's head.

Most bats have short tails. A few have long tails. But wrinkle-faced bats have no tails.

Bats' wings are made of their extra long fingers and **forelimb** bones that support thin, **elastic membranes**. Two membranes, top and bottom, are sandwiched together over the bones on each wing.

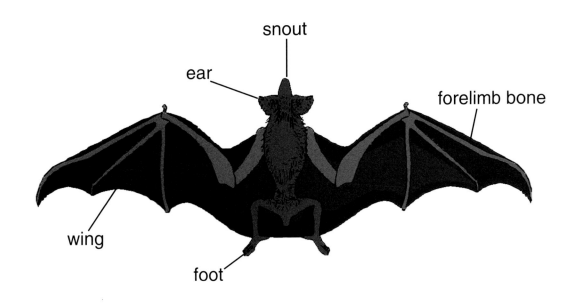

snout

ear

forelimb bone

wing

foot

*Most bats share the same features, but wrinkle-faced bats have no tails.*

# SENSES

Wrinkle-faced bats have the same five senses as humans. Like over half of all bat **species**, they also use **echolocation** to "see" in the dark.

Most bats that use echolocation send out squeaks or clicks through their mouths. But some, like the leaf-nosed bats, send noises out through their nostrils. Wrinkle-faced bats also use echolocation to "talk" to each other.

# HOW ECHOLOCATION WORKS

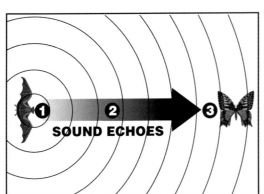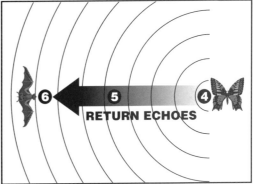

*The bat sends out sound echoes (1). These echoes travel in all directions through the air (2). The sound echoes reach an object in the bat's path (3), then bounce off it (4). The return echoes travel through the air (5) and reach the bat (6). These echoes let the bat know where the object is, how large it is, and how fast it is moving.*

# DEFENSE

Because they are small, wrinkle-faced bats are "bite-sized" for many different **predators**. Cats, dogs, raccoons, and skunks eat bats. So do owls, hawks, falcons, snakes, and large frogs. Large spiders eat bats that get caught in their webs. Even worse, some bats eat other bats! The bat's best defense against predators is to fly away.

Most bats are **nocturnal**, which means they fly at night, avoiding many predators that hunt by day. Bats also find safe, dark places to hide during the day when they **roost**. Wrinkle-faced bats, like most bats, have dark colors that make it hard for predators to see them at night.

*Wrinkle-faced bats' dark colors make it hard for predators to see them at night.*

# FOOD

Like many other bats, wrinkle-faced bats feed on the soft, mushy parts of fruits such as bananas and **pawpaws**. They suck the fruit into their mouths. They have many small bumps on the skin between their lips and gum line through which they strain the soft fruit as they feed.

*Like many other bats, wrinkle-faced bats feed on fruit.*
*This is a dog-faced bat eating a banana.*

# BABIES

Wrinkle-faced bats **breed** once or twice a year. They have one baby each time.

The baby bats are very big when they are born. They often weigh 25 percent of their mother's weight. Mother bats take good care of their babies.

Since bats fly, most people think bats are birds that lay eggs. But since bats are **mammals**, their babies are born live.

*Wrinkle-faced bats breed once or twice a year,*
*having one baby each time.*

# GLOSSARY

**BREED** - To produce young; also, a kind or type.

**CONTINENT** (KAHN-tih-nent) - One of the 7 main land masses: Europe, Asia, Africa, North America, South America, Australia and Antarctica.

**ECHOLOCATION** (ek-o-lo-KAY-shun) - The use of sound waves to find objects.

**ELASTIC** (ee-LAS-tik) - Able to return to its normal shape after being stretched or bent.

**FORELIMB** - A front limb of an animal.

**MAMMALS** (MAM-elz) - Animals with backbones that nurse their young.

**MEMBRANES** (MEM-branz) - Thin, easily bent layers of animal tissue.

**NOCTURNAL** (nok-TUR-nul) - Active by night.

**PAWPAW** - A North American tree of the custard-apple family with purple flowers and a yellow fruit.

**POLAR REGIONS** - Of or near the North or South Pole.

**PREDATOR** (PRED-uh-tor) - An animal that eats other animals.

**ROOST** - A place, such as a cave or tree, where bats rest during the day; also, to perch.

**SPECIES** (SPEE-seas) - A kind or type.

**WING SPAN** - The distance from the tip of one outstretched wing to the other.

# Index

# BIBLIOGRAPHY

Fenton, M. Brock. *Bats.* Facts On File, Inc., 1992.

Findley, James S. *Bats, A Community Perspective.* Cambridge University Press, 1993.

Johnson, Sylvia A. *The World Of Bats.* Lerner Publications Company, 1985.

Nowak, Ronald M. *Walker's Bats Of The World.* The Johns Hopkins University Press, 1994.